THE
MAKING
OF A
MAN

How Men and Boys Honor God
and Live with Integrity

TIM BROWN

with

JUDSON POLING

W PUBLISHING GROUP

AN IMPRINT OF THOMAS NELSON

Published in Nashville, Tennessee, by W Publishing, an imprint of Thomas Nelson.

Author is represented by the literary agency of Alive Communications, Inc., 7680 Goddard Street, Suite 200, Colorado Springs, CO 80920.

Thomas Nelson titles may be purchased in bulk for educational, business, fund-raising, or sales promotional use. For information, please e-mail SpecialMarkets@ ThomasNelson.com.

ISBN 978-0-529-11304-7

Cover design: Kristen Vasgaard
Cover photo: © Tom Hussey, Tom Hussey Photography
Interior photo: © paulista / Bigstock®
Interior illustrations: Beth Shagene
Interior design: Beth Shagene

First Printing July 2014 / Printed in the United States of America
HB 01.19.2024

THE
MAKING
OF A
MAN

Contents

How to Use This Guide

GROUP SIZE

The Making of a Man video curriculum is designed to be experienced in a group setting such as a Bible study, Sunday school class, or any small group gathering. After viewing the video together, members will participate in a group discussion. Ideally, this group should be no larger than fifteen people. If the total number of participants in your group is much larger, consider breaking into two or more groups.

MATERIALS NEEDED

Each participant should have his own study guide, which includes video teaching notes, small group discussion questions, and personal study to deepen learning between sessions.

TIMING

There is enough material for each session to last an hour — approximately 20 minutes for the video and 40 minutes for opening remarks, discussion, and closing prayer. If you have a longer meeting, you may wish to allow more time for discussion and activities.

SESSION FORMAT

Each session of the study guide includes the following group components:

- "Get Together" — an icebreaker question that relates to the session topic and invites input from every group member
- "Get Thinking" — the session video presentation with an outline of its key points for group members to follow along and take notes if they wish
- "Get Talking" — several group discussion questions based on the video presentation
- "Get Insight" — several more group discussion questions centering on Bible passages pertinent to the session topic
- "Get Going" — personal and/or group application activities designed to help group members interact with the session's teachings in practical, spiritually-stretching ways

Additionally, each session concludes with a "Between-Sessions Personal Study" section that includes further Bible exploration as well as recommended reading from *The Making of a Man* book.

FACILITATION

Each group should appoint a facilitator who is responsible for starting the video and for keeping track of time during discussions and activities. Facilitators may also read questions aloud and monitor discussions, prompting participants to respond and ensuring that everyone has the opportunity to participate.

PERSONAL STUDY

You can maximize the impact of the course with additional study between the group sessions. Carving out about an hour per session for personal study should be adequate; though you can complete it all in one sitting, we recommend spreading it out over a few sittings to give yourself time to process what you're studying. If you are unable to finish (or even start!) your between-sessions study, still attend the group study video session! We are all busy and life happens.

Note: In session two, the group is going to participate in an activity that requires a large bowl of water and identical books of matches for every group member but the facilitator. Designate one person to be responsible for bringing these supplies to the group meeting.

A Man Uses
His Talents

GET TOGETHER

If the men in your group are just meeting each other for the first time, be sure to go around the circle and introduce yourselves to each other. Have each group member complete the following icebreaker sentence:

As a boy, I wanted to grow up to be a _____,

because _____

_____.

GET THINKING

Watch the video for session one. Use the outline provided to note any thoughts or concepts that stand out to you.

NOTES

Tim Brown made the transition from being a Heisman Trophy college star to playing in the NFL. A 97-yard kickoff return in his first game boosted his confidence — though he quickly discovered that the professional players he encountered were faster, stronger, and more talented than in college.

After his first season, Tim was named to the Pro Bowl as a kick returner. When he returned home, his parents welcomed him with a big banner across the porch to congratulate him. However, his mother told him to leave the "big head" outside and just be "Timmy" when he got inside!

We all have talents, but we need to use our skills and abilities for God's glory, not our own.

Jesus told a parable about a man who gave his three servants bags of gold to use in his absence. The first two used theirs well to increase their master's wealth. The third one foolishly did nothing with the treasure entrusted to him. The point is clear: God wants us to use the talents He has given us and not hide them away.

You may think God can't use your abilities for Him, or you may not know what your God-given skills are. However, when you're in tune with God, and are reading the Bible and praying, you're in a position to get the answers you need.

You may not have the talents others have, but that's okay. Maybe you have the ability to listen well, or multitask, or find solutions to complex problems. God has entrusted you with those skills, and He wants you to use them for His glory.

"I mean to make myself a man, and if I succeed in that, I shall succeed in everything else."

**Attributed to
President James A. Garfield**

WORTH REPEATING

"Every boy dreams about growing up to be his vision of a man."

"No matter what gifts or abilities we have been given, we need to use those skills for God's glory."

"Whatever your talents are, embrace them. Don't dig a hole and hide them in the ground. God has given those skills to you for a reason, even if you can't see it right now."

GET TALKING

Tim Brown points out that we men are on a journey to understand what we need to do to make ourselves into the men that God wants each of us to be. Our search for understanding manhood begins early in life. As boys, we received ideas from a variety of sources: television, movies, books, sports figures, and, of course, our dads. Sometimes, we learned what we *didn't* want to become by watching men. Most of us can identify a man — in real-life or someone whom we learned about — who stood out, who impressed us, and whom we wanted to be like.

1. Share with the group members a man who was a hero for you growing up. What was it about him that made him your hero?

"Show me the man you honor, and I will know what kind of a man you are, for it shows me what your ideal of manhood is, and what kind of a man you long to be."

Thomas Carlyle

---

2. Without naming names, describe a bad example of manhood you encountered in your formative years. How has that man continued to affect you — for good or bad — even now?

3. If someone was your hero, he no doubt had some skills or special abilities he used to make the world a better place. He may have only affected those in his immediate family, or he may have been famous and changed history. In addition, heroes are almost always men of exemplary character, not just talent. All of our abilities vary, but true heroes live with integrity, compassion, and a drive to make a difference. What is it about a person who has talent *without* character that makes him unworthy to emulate?

4. Given that "bad" men do so much harm, what do you think fuels our society's fascination with men who flaunt their destructive lifestyles and live with lax morals?

"It is a grand mistake to think of being great without goodness; and I pronounce it as certain, that there never was yet a truly great man that was not at the same time truly virtuous."

Benjamin Franklin

GET INSIGHT

Because we are all human and made in God's image, we all have a longing for fulfillment and to find a purpose that can carry us through the ups and downs of life. We all want love and respect and to be treated fairly by others. We all feel emotions: *sadness* when something valuable is lost; *angry* when we are blocked from something we want; *fearful* when threatened; and *happy* when good things come our way. We also all have faculties of reason to help us solve problems and make good decisions.

The same God who made us to have so much in common also made us to have differences. Other than twins, no two people have ever had the same genetic code; and even identical twins are never exactly alike in temperament, interests, and abilities. These differences among us don't make one person better than another — in fact, quite the contrary, for they make us interdependent. When we recognize our differences as being God-given, it instills a sense of respect and of valuing one another.

5. **Read** Psalm 139:13 – 14. When are you most likely not to respect yourself or others as "fearfully and wonderfully made" by God?

6. Although you may feel like you are bragging as you answer this question, what God-given abilities do you possess that you feel responsible to use well?

Why is accurately knowing and faithfully using your God-given talents so important?

7. Read Matthew 25:14 – 30. In the Parable of the Talents (mentioned by Tim in the video), the foolish servant did nothing productive with the money he was given. It kind of makes you wonder, doesn't it? Why would someone do such a wasteful thing?

8. The problem wasn't that the man thought he could "get away with it" or that the master wouldn't hold him accountable for making good investments. The real reason is quite different. What was the servant's assessment of his boss? What kind of man and leader did the servant believe his master was?

9. It's obvious that the master represents God and the servants represent us and our varied responses to God. The foolish servant's problem was not that he was lazy; it was that he didn't believe his master had legitimate rights over him, nor did he believe he was just and worthy of loyalty. That being the case, how do you think a wrong view of what God is like — believing He is a tyrant and unreasonable — will affect a person's fruitfulness and willingness to serve Him?

In what ways do you think *your* view of God affects how you use — or don't use — your gifts?

GET GOING

What are your strengths? How might God want to use them for His work?

Marcus Buckingham has noted that strengths are not just things you do well but things that, when you do them, make you feel strong. Defining strengths that way makes an important distinction: you might be *good* at doing something, but if it drains you and makes you feel weak, it is not technically a strength. You could rightly call it an *ability*, but such a skill is not one of your strengths.

Conversely, the things you do with near perfect performance every time you do them are your strengths — as long as you feel strong when you do them. Yes, you might be tired afterward, but with some rest, you're ready to get back into the fray. You actually *derive* energy from your strengths. You might even be a beginner at something, but if you're consistently drawn to that activity — if you feel *strong* when you do it, no matter your skill level — consider that a strength as well.

Like the master in the parable, God gave you strengths — some of which you know and some of which you may have yet to discover. He wants you to use what He's given you for His work in the world. When you are the best version of *you*, living out of your Spirit-empowered strengths, you can be confident you are doing the work God has for you. Tim Brown's main strength was athletic ability — and you may identify with that strength. Or you might have an aptitude for administration, or entrepreneurship, or you may possess artistic skill. Your strength may not look like anyone else's, but that's okay. Whatever God leads you to do with your strengths is right for you, because those accomplishments flow out of His design for you and are meant for His glory.

This week, keep a "strengths/weakness" journal. Use the chart below or create your own on a separate sheet of paper. Each day at lunch, dinner, and just before bed, jot down anything you did that made you feel strong and anything that made you feel weak. At the end of the week, summarize what you think are your top strengths — and consider how you can do activities that involve those strengths to a greater degree. Also, summarize what seem to be your weaknesses. How can you do less of those activities?

I felt strong when I . . .	I felt weak when I . . .

After making observations for one week, summarize your findings below.

My top strengths to lean into:	My top weakness to avoid:

To conclude this meeting, pair up with another person. Pray that you can know and use your gifts, talents, and strengths for God's work. Pray that God will bring to light any "buried" strengths you have and confirm the ones you already know. Ask God to show you specific people or situations where your gifts and strengths are needed.

Between-Sessions Personal Study

Complete the following personal study on your own sometime between now and your next group meeting. It's best to not try to finish it all at once but do it over a few sittings to give yourself time to mull over what you're studying.

READ AND REFLECT

Read chapter 4, "A Man Uses His Skills," and chapter 7, "Even Heisman Winners Get Humbled," in *The Making of a Man* book. Use the space below to write any key points or questions you want to bring to the next group meeting.

REVIEW AND STUDY

1. Look over the video outline and your notes from the group study. What is the "big idea" you want to take away? It may be a quote, a new way of looking at an issue, a reminder of a forgotten lesson, or something you sense God wants you to do. Note it here:

2. During the group time, you shared about someone who was a hero for you growing up. **Read** Psalm 16:2 – 3. This passage points out that God is our leader — and the supreme good in our lives who gives us all the other good things we have. It also says we should seek to delight in good *people*. As the *New Living Translation* puts it, "The godly people in the land are my true heroes!"

In what ways do you think the hero you mentioned from your childhood is also a gift from God?

Did that person give you a model of godly character? If so, describe those traits. If not, what was missing?

Why do you think God needs to remind us, as fully grown men, that we still need heroes who are strong believers (compare Philippians 2:29 – 30)?

In what area of your life could you use a strong, godly example? What's a step you could take to seek out such a person?

3. Being a man means, obviously, being human. But being a man in the sense of this study also involves being *masculine*. In order to strive toward being good men, we must also have a clear understanding of what it means to be masculine.

What are some of the superficial characteristics of "manhood" that everybody just assumes are true?

In light of what you just wrote, fill in the following chart:

Ways Jesus fits the masculine stereotype	Ways Jesus is not like the masculine stereotype
Ways I fit the masculine stereotype	**Ways I am not like the masculine stereotype**

MASCULINITY AND MANHOOD

"There are two ways to define manhood. One way is to say that manhood is the opposite of womanhood. The other is to say that manhood is the opposite of childhood ... A child is self-centered, fearful, and dependent. A man is bold, courageous, respectful, independent, and of service to others. Thus a man becomes a man when he matures and leaves behind childish things."

Brett and Kate McKay, *The Art of Manliness*

"Masculinity is not something given to you, but something you gain. And you gain it by winning small battles with honor."

Norman Mailer

"No man is more unhappy than he who never faces adversity. For he is not permitted to prove himself."

Seneca

"It is not necessary for a man to be actively bad in order to make a failure in life; simple inaction will accomplish it. Nature has everywhere written her protest against idleness; everything which ceases to struggle, which remains inactive, rapidly deteriorates. It is the struggle toward an ideal, the constant effort to get higher and further, which develops manhood and character."

James Terry White

"A man is not merely a man but a man among men, in a world of men. Being good at being a man has more to do with a man's ability to succeed with men than it does with a man's relationship to any woman or any group of women. When someone tells a man to be a man, they are telling him to be more like other men, more like the majority of men, and ideally more like the men who other men hold in high regard."

Jack Donovan

4. Read 1 Corinthians 13:11, 14:20, and 16:13. In what ways do you think manhood is the opposite of womanhood (that is, masculine versus feminine)? In what ways is it the opposite of childhood (that is, masculine versus immature)?

What values do you see taught (or shown by example) in the following passages that line up with the idea that our manhood and maturity are developed through endurance, perseverance, and intentionally seeking challenging situations that will test us?

• Matthew 4:1

• 1 Peter 1:6 – 7

• James 1:2 – 4

• Proverbs 27:17

5. Jewish boys are brought into the full rights and blessings of manhood at age thirteen through a ritual known as Bar Mitzvah. Many tribal societies have a similar "coming of age" or initiation experience for young boys, such as the Xhosa tribe's Ukwaluka ceremony that Nelson Mandela went through at age sixteen. What is noteworthy about these passages to manhood is that the young man must prove himself through some kind of ordeal before he can become one of the men who have responsibility for the tribe.

How do you think gangs supply a substitute "tribal initiation" for some young men today? What other kinds of initiation are taking the place of this widely practiced ritual (which is absent from our modern society)?

6. In what ways do you think men can help "sharpen" each other? In particular, how do you think older men should be sharpening younger men (similar to the positive ways men in tribal societies do so)?

7. If you were to design a Christian men's initiation process that was intended to help young men cross the line to manhood and be welcomed into the community of older Christian men, what would you include?

8. Read Matthew 5:14 – 16. Jesus wants our good deeds to shine so that God gets the glory. As Tim Brown pointed out, to fully function as a man, you have to use your talents for God's glory as well.

In what ways do some of your talents (and resultant good deeds) still remain "under a bushel/basket"?

What is one step you can take to let your light shine more brightly?

SESSION 2

A Man Overcomes Temptation

GET TOGETHER

> *Note:* During this session, the group is going to participate in an activity that requires a large bowl of water and identical books of matches for everyone but the facilitator. Designate one person to be responsible for bringing these supplies to the group meeting.

GET TOGETHER

Begin your time together by sharing your response to the following icebreaker question:

What were the circumstances around your first romantic kiss? Describe to the group.

GET THINKING

Watch the video for session two. Use the outline provided to note any thoughts or concepts that stand out to you.

NOTES

At age sixteen, Tim started dating a girl with whom he eventually had sex. This began a pattern that carried on through college of him ignoring God's command not to have sex before marriage.

Tim rationalized his giving into temptation — the girls were beautiful, and it happened so easily, so why fight it?

The Bible is clear: "It is God's will that you should be sanctified: that you should avoid sexual immorality" (1 Thessalonians 4:3). Sexual temptation is a big problem for most men — and both the media and cultural norms make it even harder.

God wants to help. Paul writes, "No temptation has overtaken you except what is common to mankind. And God is faithful; he will not let you be tempted beyond what you can bear. But when you are tempted, he will also provide a way out so that you can endure it" (1 Corinthians 10:13).

In the Bible, Joseph is a great example of a man who resisted temptation. Despite Potiphar's wife taking a liking to him, he resisted her advances. He even ended up in jail falsely accused of attempted rape.

We must flee tempting situations. Paul writes, "Flee the evil desires of youth" (2 Timothy 2:22). We can't help it when we notice a beautiful woman, but we can choose where our eyes go next.

We must let women know where we stand — flashing our wedding ring if we're married; telling our dates we want relationships that start with friendship, not sex; staying out of tempting situations. We must also train our brains to focus on topics other than sex.

A single victory gives us confidence to do it again. Over time, we form a habit. This works with other temptations: Take control of your eyes and mind. Don't even crack the door to temptation. Look for the way out that God provides.

Tim eventually realized he was separated from God, and he reached the end of his rebellion. He prayed to God, asked for His help, and committed to be a spiritual man — not a natural man.

> "The serpent is helpless unless he finds an apple to work with."
> **George Ade**

We need to live God's way. Paul writes, "Walk by the Spirit, and you will not gratify the desires of the flesh" (Galatians 5:16). The Holy Spirit will take charge.

WORTH REPEATING

"We're visual creatures. We're wired to enjoy looking at beautiful women."

"A single victory with your eyes or mind over sexual temptation can give you the confidence to do it again the next time."

"You can win the battle against temptation, but you can't do it in your own strength. The good news is that when you have God in your life, you have extra ammunition for the battle."

GET TALKING

1. When you were growing up, what values about sex were you taught?

2. During your teen years, how did God fit into your understanding of the purpose of sex (if at all)?

3. How do you think Christians can affirm the dangers of sexual activity outside the bounds of marriage, and yet at the same time not make it sound as if Christianity teaches that sex is bad?

4. Many men believe that if you don't actually have sex with another woman, there is no harm in looking at (and lusting after) her. How do you respond to this common perspective?

"God is better served in resisting a temptation to evil than in many formal prayers."
William Penn

5. According to the following 1 – 10 scale, rate (by circling) your own "temptability" when it comes to sex.

1 2	3 4	5 6	7 8	9 10
Not a big deal	I sometimes feel mild temptation	I notice women frequently	I really struggle to maintain purity	I am (or think I might be) a sex addict

GET INSIGHT

The Bible is surprisingly frank in its teaching about sexuality, temptation, and the ways we as men can fall prey to our desires. One such passage is Proverbs 7:6 – 23, in which a wise older man looks out his window to see a younger man heading to the wrong side of town. There he meets up with a married woman with whom he has a tryst. The observer makes several astute comments that serve as a lesson for us all.

6. Read the Proverbs passage aloud in the group. What time of day does this scene take place? Where is the young man when he faces his temptation?

What do you think is the significance of including those details? How do those circumstances affect your own "temptability"?

7. Although the woman in the story is a willing partner, the young man is the one described as a fool. What do you see as especially foolish about his actions?

> "Every conquering temptation represents a new fund of moral energy. Every trial endured and weathered in the right spirit makes a soul nobler and stronger than it was before."
>
> **William Butler Yeats**

8. Verse 22 says that he follows her "all at once" — as if this action is a sudden impulse, almost by accident. In reality, how did the young man set himself up for a fall? How do we play similar tricks on ourselves in this area of our lives?

GROUP ACTIVITY:
Can You Take the Heat?

At this point, distribute to each man except for the facilitator a book of identical matches (all the same length). Place a large bowl of water in the midst of the men where all can reach it. Put down your study guide and hold only the matches as the facilitator reads the following directions:

> *You are now going to engage in a test of your true manhood called, "Can You Take the Heat?" You each have a book of matches. The goal is to find out who has "what it takes," because*

you are going to hold a matchstick between your fingers to see who can hang onto it the longest. Once you blow out the flame or drop the match in this bowl of water, you are done. The man who lasts the longest is the winner.

Okay, everybody take out one match and hold it against the strike area. On the count of three, we're going to all begin at exactly the same time. Because the matches are all the same length, there's no unfair advantage to any man.

Everybody ready? I will be the judge of who holds on the longest. On the count of three we will begin. One ... two ... three!

Afterward, the facilitator will declare the winner or call a draw. Then, debrief the activity with the following questions:

1. How much did the set-up language about "testing your true manhood" and "having what it takes" figure into how much longer you were willing to hold a lit match than you normally would?

2. How does our desire as men to fit in, compete, or engage in risk-taking lead us to sometimes exercise bad judgment?

9. Read Proverbs 6:27 – 29. In your own words, what do you think this proverb is trying to say?

Naturally, if you don't want to get burned, don't hold a match! Or, better yet, don't even light it. Notice that nowhere in the instructions were you explicitly told to light the match! You could have followed the rules and won by just holding an unlit match. (Maybe someone figured that out or read ahead in this lesson and discovered that possibility!)

Notice how peer pressure, a picture of a lit match, the bowl of water, and suggestive language all factored into what you chose to do — though you could have easily done otherwise. This same thing happens in our culture all the time. What is considered "normal" sexual morality bombards us from every corner. Often that accepted conduct falls far short of God's standards, and yet we get pulled into following the crowd. For example, it is commonplace for casual dating to involve sex — instead of getting to know the person before knowing each other's body. It is also accepted that couples will live together — instead of committing to marriage before having sex. Affairs are portrayed in the entertainment world as if they don't seem to hurt people all that much — instead of showing an honest picture of the pain of ruined marriages, wounded children, STDs, and the high cost of a lust-fueled lifestyle.

According to Proverbs 6:27 – 29, real men guard themselves from taking foolish risks and live by principle rather than peer pressure. Yet for many of us, being a "real man" means doing really dumb stuff so we can appear cool to those around us!

10. What lesson do you want to take away from this match activity for yourself? How would you like to put that into practice in the coming days?

GET GOING

Take a few moments to think through how you want to guard yourself against sexual sin. Use the diagram below as a guide, and take notes on it.

After you have filled in each section, pair up with another man and share what you wrote. Close in prayer for each other, asking God to help you remain sexually pure and be an example to others of the benefits of living within the freedom of God's moral safeguards.

How I Will Protect My Mind	How I Will Protect My Marriage (or Future Marriage)
The Cost of Sexual Sin	The Benefits of Sexual Purity

Between-Sessions Personal Study

Complete the following personal study on your own sometime between now and your next group meeting. It's best to not try to finish it all at once but do it over a few sittings to give yourself time to mull over what you're studying.

READ AND REFLECT

Read chapter 5, "Persistence Creates Confidence," chapter 10, "A Man Overcomes Temptation," and chapter 11, "Faith Is for Life," in *The Making of a Man* book. Use the space below to write any key points or questions you want to bring to the next group meeting.

REVIEW AND STUDY

1. Look over the video outline and your notes from the group study. What is the "big idea" you want to take away? It may be a quote, a new way of looking at an issue, a reminder of a forgotten lesson, or something you sense God wants you to do. Note that below:

2. Returning to Proverbs 7:6 – 23, a passage you looked at briefly during the meeting, note in the following verses what the woman does to make herself alluring to the young man. (You will need to make some generalizations based on her specific actions or words and translate some of the customs into what might be contemporary counterparts.)

• Verse 10

• Verse 11

• Verse 13

• Verse 15

• Verses 16 – 17

• Verse 18

• Verse 21

Which of these actions would appeal to you if a woman approached you in that manner?

What other actions or words from an attractive woman might tempt you?

3. In your own words, what fallout would you expect to receive from being unfaithful to your wife in each of the following areas? (Or, if that has already happened, what was the cost?)

• Effect on my wife:

• Effect on my kids:

• Effect on my extended family:

• Effect on my close friends:

• Effect on the other woman:

(cont.)

• Effect on people in her world:

• Effect on my church:

• Effect on non-Christians who know me:

• Effect on the reputation of Christ:

• Effect on my relationship with God:

• Effect on me:

"Temptation is the devil
looking through the keyhole.
Yielding is opening the door
and inviting him in."
Billy Sunday

4. Now complete the sentence below. Give careful thought to your words and come up with as many details as possible. If you *have* had an affair, use both the actual reasons from the past and any other reasons you might now give if you were to repeat that act.

Despite all this potential damage, if I ever had an affair, it would be because I ...

5. Read 2 Corinthians 10:5 and Job 31:1. Practically speaking, how can a man in this day and age actually do what these verses say to do?

6. Read Proverbs 5:15 – 20. Based on these verses, what is your impression of God's attitude toward sex within marriage?

How can this perspective help you in your fight against temptation?

7. While many men have felt the shame and regret of an affair, even more men are ensnared by readily available Internet pornography. Rate your own struggles in this area using the 1 – 10 scale below:

1 2	3 4	5 6	7 8	9 10
Not a big deal	I am occasionally tempted	I give in to porn from time to time	This is a frequent struggle	My sexual habits are out of control

Where would you *like* to be on the above scale? What do you think will help you get there?

8. Regardless of the area of your life in which temptation is strongest, none of us can successfully fight a spiritual battle on our own. What advice does Proverbs 11:14 give in this regard?

Who are your counselors/advisers that help you in the area of temptation most troublesome to you?

9. Read James 5:16. What additional action does this verse encourage us to take?

What good do you think will come from telling someone about your struggles?

SESSION 3

A Man Takes
Responsibility

GET TOGETHER

Begin your time together by sharing your response to the following icebreaker question:

What's a crazy, irresponsible thing you did as a teenager that you can laugh at now?

GET THINKING

Watch the video for session three. Use the outline provided to note any thoughts or concepts that stand out to you.

NOTES

Just before graduation from college, Tim found out his girlfriend was pregnant. His son, Taylor, was born the next January.

Tim wanted to take responsibility and make sure he provided for his son, so he moved Taylor and Taylor's mom to live near him in Dallas.

"The price of greatness is responsibility."

Winston Churchill

Men today have a huge problem taking responsibility. This goes all the way back to the Garden of Eden when Adam blamed Eve — and even God — for his disobedience! Later, during the Exodus, Aaron didn't take responsibility for the golden calf incident. Perhaps worst of all is when King David worked double-time to cover up his affair.

When Tim picked the wrong room during his junior year at college, he was not allowed to make a change. It taught him he needed to deal with his pride and fallibility.

The prophet Nathan helped King David take responsibility for his actions. We also need quality friends in our lives who we can confide in, who will advise us, and who want to share both good times and bad.

Chester McGlockton was that kind of friend to Tim. Although their relationship got off to a rocky start, when they both committed their lives to Christ, it created a strong bond between them. Chester was the one who introduced Tim to Sherice, the woman who later became his wife. He also encouraged Tim spiritually and made sure he was always treating his wife, kids, and extended family right.

Sharing your problems and being accountable to a godly friend is a huge blessing. These kinds of friends make it easier to live a successful life and own up to your responsibilities as a man.

WORTH REPEATING

"Many men today have a huge problem with taking responsibility for their actions."

"When you make a mistake, you have to deal with the fallout. That means confessing what you've done, doing what you can to repair it, and accepting the result."

"Sharing your problems and being accountable to a godly friend is a huge blessing. When you surround yourself with these kinds of people, you'll find it a whole lot easier to live a successful life and own up to your responsibilities as a man."

GET TALKING

1. Tim Brown believes that men today have a big problem with taking responsibility. How would you rate yourself as far as being a man who is generally willing to take responsibility for his actions?

2. What do you think explains the perception — or reality — that men have a major problem in this area?

During this session, Tim talked about the significance of his relationship with Chester McGlockton and how much a good friend's honesty and blunt challenges meant to him. But many of us men get defensive when a friend tries to point out an area of inconsistency or questions our behavior. We either think personal matters are just that — *personal* — and nobody's business but our own, or we feel judged and shamed, and so we resist the input because of how bad we feel.

The flip side is that many of us don't want to say hard things like that to a friend — it spoils the fun of the relationship, and we fear rejection. Besides, we know we have our own faults, so who are we to comment on anybody else's life? We should be working on the log in our own eye and not pointing out the speck in a brother's eye!

3. How easy is it for you to have someone give you critical feedback about your personal life or conduct?

How do you think you compare with other men in this regard? (If you are really bold, ask the men who are sitting with you if your assessment of yourself is accurate!)

> "Do not judge me by my successes, judge me by how many times I fell down and got back up again."
> **Nelson Mandela**

4. Think about a time when someone came to you — or you went to someone else — and offered needed but hard-to-hear feedback about an area of personal conduct or failure to take responsibility. What made that hard? What was the eventual outcome?

GET INSIGHT

In Genesis 3, we have the first instance of human sin — Adam and Eve ate from the forbidden tree that was in the Garden of Eden. We also have the first instance of how humans typically respond to wrongdoing: hiding (literally among the bushes), covering (with fig-leaves), and blaming (Adam speaks more of others than himself).

5. Read Genesis 3:8 – 13. Technically, when Adam spoke to God after eating the fruit, everything he said was "truth" — he did not lie. So what untruths are implied in his words (for example, who does he seem to want to blame)? What truths should have been included?

"Every excuse I ever heard
made perfect sense to the
person who made it."

Dr. Daniel T. Drubin

In your own words, what responses should Adam and Eve have given?

6. The Bible stresses how important relationships are for the formation of our character — both for good and for bad. **Read** 1 Corinthians 15:33 and 1 Peter 4:3 – 4, which show how the wrong crowd can corrupt us. Recall a situation in your life when your behaviors were strongly influenced by being involved with "the wrong crowd" and you now regret your actions.

Now recall a situation when you stood against what others were attempting to lure you to do and you're glad you went the right direction.

What factors caused you to go along with the wrong actions in the first example? What factors enabled you to resist in the second?

7. By contrast, the right kind of friends can do wonders for building our character. **Read** 1 Samuel 23:15 – 16. In this story, David was being persecuted and Jonathan came to his aid. What do you think is the difference between "helping a friend" and "helping a friend find strength in God" (verse 16), as Jonathan did for David?

"Love always involves responsibility, and love always involves sacrifice."

William Barclay

What might it look like to have this kind of relationship in your life?

GET GOING

Do a quick relationship inventory by filling out "the State of My Relational World" form that follows. Note that some names may come up more than once.

THE STATE OF MY RELATIONAL WORLD
Buddies of mine I hang out with, but it doesn't go much beyond that ...
Men who I used to be close to but who have drifted away (or the relationship ended painfully) ...
Long-term friends (ten-plus years) who are very important to me ...
Recently acquired friends who have great potential to become significant ...
Men with whom I would like to have a closer friendship ...
Men of character who know me well and do not fear challenging me to take responsibility ...

Pair up with another man in the group. Share together any reactions you had to doing this inventory (go into as much or little detail as you choose), and what you think God might want you to do as a result of this study. Pray for each other to faithfully follow through how God is leading.

Between-Sessions Personal Study

Complete the following personal study and reflection on your own sometime between now and your next group meeting. It's best to not try to finish it all at once but do it over a few sittings to give yourself time to mull over what you're studying.

READ AND REFLECT

Read chapter 8, "A Man Takes Responsibility," and chapter 14, "Surround Yourself with Good People," in *The Making of a Man* book. Use the space below to write any key points or questions you want to bring to the next group meeting.

REVIEW AND STUDY

1. Look over the video outline and your notes from the group study. What is the "big idea" you want to take away? It may be a quote, a new way of looking at an issue, a reminder of a forgotten lesson, or something you sense God wants you to do. Note that here:

2. In your own words, what does it mean to be a man of integrity?

Who has modeled integrity for you? What do you appreciate about that person?

What is an area of your life where you would like to have more integrity?

3. Read Psalm 15. This psalm describes several qualities of a person who can stand before a holy God and not be afraid. According to verse 4, what does it mean for someone to "swear to his own hurt" (NASB) or "keep promises even when it hurts" (NLT)?

What factors cause your resolve to weaken when it comes to keeping your promises? What helps you stay strong?

4. Sometimes we have trouble keeping our word because we shouldn't have given it in the first place — we would have been better off saying no to the request. What is an example of something you wish you wouldn't have promised to do?

What makes it hard for you to say no sometimes?

5. Read Luke 4:42 – 43. What request was made of Jesus, to which he said no?

Obviously, what those people wanted was a "good" thing and a reasonable request, but Jesus said no anyway. What do you suppose was their reaction?

What can you learn from Jesus' decision-making process to help you when you need to say no?

"What is the biggest obstacle facing the family right now? It is overcommitment; time pressure. There is nothing that will destroy family life more insidiously than hectic schedules and busy lives ... If Satan can't make you sin, he'll make you busy, and that's just about the same thing."

Dr. James Dobson

---

6. A big part of our character is shaped — for good or bad — by the company we keep. In particular, it seems rare to have the kind of men in our lives who can say hard things. It's also rare for us not to be defensive when a brother in Christ admonishes us. However, we are not being a good friend if we give a pass to someone who needs to be challenged.

Read Proverbs 27:6. How would you put this verse into your own words?

Why do you think the actions of friends can seem like wounds?

Why do you think enemies figuratively "kiss" you?

Think of a friend who needs you to step up enough to "wound" him. How can you do that in love so there is only healing and not needless pain?

7. **Read** Proverbs 27:17. Imagine that if instead of two pieces of iron, you had one piece of iron and one piece of wood.

What kind of relationship would you have if those items represented two kinds of men?

How do you think someone who is too soft can learn to be more of a man of iron?

In what way do you need to become more solid and iron-like?

8. **Read** Galatians 6:2–5. What does it mean to "bear [carry] one another's burdens" (NKJV)?

Verse 5 says to "bear [carry] your own load" (NKJV). What do you think that means?

How do you reconcile the apparent contradiction between verse 5 and verse 2?

A Man Forgives
Others

GET TOGETHER

Begin your time together by having each group member complete the following icebreaker sentence:

You might be surprised to know that one of my pet peeves is

_____.

GET THINKING

Watch the video for session four. Use the outline provided to note any thoughts or concepts that stand out to you.

___
NOTES

Eugene Brown, Tim's father, was the oldest of ten kids and had to quit school to work to support his family. He had an amazing work ethic and was good at fixing things, but he didn't want Tim to have to labor with his hands like he had to do.

Eugene's work schedule kept him from spending time with his kids. Tim has only a couple of memories of doing something with just his dad: one was going fishing, and the other was his dad's crazy scheme to get Tim into modeling.

One time when Tim was thirteen, his dad came home late and they got into a fight. His dad threatened to kill him and went out to the car to get his gun. Tim's mom calmed down his father and a crisis was averted.

However, the incident changed Tim and his father's relationship. No one talked about it, but inside Tim was torn up.

Jesus warned about the damage that unforgiveness can cause. In one parable, he told about a servant who owed a king a large amount, but the king forgave the debt. However, that servant mistreated someone who owed him a relatively small amount. The servant should have shown the kind of mercy he himself had received.

Because we've been forgiven our great debt to God through Christ's death on the cross, we need to forgive others. Paul writes, "Be kind and compassionate to one another, forgiving each other, just as in Christ God forgave you" (Ephesians 4:32).

For many years, the rift between Tim and his dad went unaddressed. Finally, Tim decided he needed to take the first step and told his dad he forgave him. He also asked for forgiveness himself. They finally became father and son again.

"Forgiveness does not change the past, but it does change the future."

Paul Boese

WORTH REPEATING

"God expects us to forgive others in the same way that He has forgiven us for our sins."

"Forgiveness is a requirement for all believers in Christ. Of course, this doesn't make it any easier to do — especially if the hurt is deep."

"If you are the one who was wronged and you are holding a grudge, ask the Lord to help you let it go ... If you are the one who has offended someone ... take responsibility for your mistakes, and ask for forgiveness."

GET TALKING

We all have a natural inclination to take revenge when someone hurts us. We often defend it as an issue of justice — we may feel as if it creates a kind of "balance" and without it something is off. One only has to look at the fifty or so armed conflicts going on in our world at this moment to see that this attitude is considered normal and justified. Doesn't every tribe or country think it is in the right? Who goes to war believing that maybe they are the bad guys? We all are prone to think, *I have a right to feel this way after what he did to me!* Whether as individuals or nations, we stubbornly maintain that retaliation will solve the problem of aggression — or at least make us feel better. Even if we don't extract the payback personally, we often wish that God would allow some misfortune to happen to those who've hurt us!

1. Give some reasons why you agree or disagree with each of the following statements:

- Those who hurt me need to feel my anger and experience painful consequences.

- I should only offer forgiveness if someone sincerely shows remorse.

- People will think I'm a pushover if I forgive others too easily.

- Forgiving others without making them pay encourages them to repeat the offenses.

If we only had to forgive people for petty offenses — cutting us off in traffic, providing slow service at a restaurant, saying stinging words — we might see the value in toning down our harsh responses and more quickly offering forgiveness. But most of us can recount a severe injustice that deeply marked us, maybe to this day. Forgiving that person seems impossible — and maybe even unwarranted. That individual has scarred us for life. How can we let him or her off the hook? On top of that, the offender may not even think he or she did anything wrong, which only rubs the salt of denial into an already painful wound.

2. What conditions make it easy to forgive others? What conditions make it hard?

3. Are you aware of anyone who still needs your forgiveness? Describe what happened and why you haven't forgiven that person.

If you cannot think of anyone you need to forgive, how did you get to that point of completely forgiving everyone in your life?

If you do know of someone you need to forgive, what would have to happen for you to be able to forgive that person?

"Resentment is like drinking poison and then hoping it will kill your enemies."

Attributed to Nelson Mandela

GET INSIGHT

4. Tim Brown referred to a parable Jesus told about a servant who was forgiven a huge debt he had but wouldn't forgive a petty debt owed to him. **Read** Matthew 18:32 – 33. What is the basis for the master expecting the servant to be merciful? Why do you suppose it didn't work in this case? Why doesn't it always work for us?

5. Now **read** Acts 7:54 – 60. What details in the story may have helped Stephen have such a willingness to forgive his executioners?

How would you make an application to your own life of what you read in this passage?

"Always forgive your enemies. Nothing annoys them so much."

Oscar Wilde

---

6. In the original Greek of the New Testament, three different words are used that are translated as our English word "forgiveness." The first word is *aphiemi*, which means to pardon, send away, or cancel a debt; the second is *charizomai*, which is derived from a root word that means "grace" and thus means to graciously give, pardon, or remit; and the third is *apoluo*, which is based on a word that means to untie, loose, annul, or release.

All of these words have in common the idea of getting rid of something and of taking an action to set your debtor — and yourself — free. How would you put in your own words the connection between freedom and forgiveness?

7. Is it acceptable to forgive someone but choose not to have a relationship after you have granted that person forgiveness? Why or why not?

8. If forgiveness leads to freedom — and freedom is such a desirable thing — why don't we do it more readily? What do we get out of not forgiving and holding a grudge?

"To forgive is to set a prisoner free and discover that the prisoner was you."

Lewis B. Smedes

GET GOING

Take a few minutes to fill out the "Two Possible Worlds" personal reflection tool below. Think about various areas of your life and imagine two different scenarios in each: (1) what it would look like if everybody resisted forgiving each other, and (2) what it would be like if everyone showed readiness to forgive. Try to list two or three points under each scenario.

TWO POSSIBLE WORLDS		
Area of Life	World #1: Resistance to Forgive	World #2: Eagerness to Forgive
Marriage		
Family		
Friendships		
Workplace		
Church		
World		

When you are done with the exercise, get together in groups of two or three for prayer. Pray that you can be part of building a world where people learn to show compassion and forgive as a way of life. Pray that you would see opportunities where you could start to do that this week.

Between-Sessions Personal Study

Complete the following personal study on your own sometime between now and your next group meeting. It's best to not try to finish it all at once but do it over a few sittings to give yourself time to mull over what you're studying.

READ AND REFLECT

Read chapter 3, "Manhood Starts with Dad," and chapter 19, "A Man Overcomes Evil," in *The Making of a Man* book. Use the space below to write any key points or questions you want to bring to the next group meeting.

REVIEW AND STUDY

1. Look over the video outline and your notes from the group study. What is the "big idea" you want to take away? It may be a quote, a new way of looking at an issue, a reminder of a forgotten lesson, or something you sense God wants you to do. Note that here:

2. In what ways have you seen unforgiveness hurt the person who is unforgiving?

3. What do you think explains our natural bent toward retaliation and payback? (Be more specific than just saying "sin"!)

"To err is human;
to forgive, divine."
Alexander Pope

4. Read Ephesians 4:26 – 27. In this passage, Paul implies that being angry is an emotion we will all feel and that we don't necessarily sin when we express it. We know that Jesus was angry at times yet he was sinless (see Mark 3:1 – 5; John 2:13 – 16), which shows that it must be possible to be angry without sinning. With that in mind, what do you think sinless anger looks like?

5. Do you think a *lack* of anger is ever sinful? Why or why not?

6. What do you think Paul means when he says, "Do not let the sun go down on your anger" (NASB)? Why do you think he added that command in this context?

7. According to verse 27, what is the opportunity the devil has when we are angry that we must not allow to happen?

"Mistakes are always forgivable, if one has the courage to admit them."
Bruce Lee

8. How do you think the devil has used your anger for his purposes? Thinking back to a specific situation, how could you have been angry in that context *without* sinning?

9. Do you think there is a connection between truly feeling your anger and truly being able to forgive? Explain.

10. Read Ephesians 4:32. What is the connection between the attitudes in the first part of the verse — being kind and tender-hearted (compassionate) — and the last part of the verse — being able to forgive? Can forgiveness ever happen without those first two qualities? Explain.

A Man Has His Priorities
in Order

GET TOGETHER

Begin your time together by sharing your response to the following icebreaker question:

Describe a time in your life when you were living with upside-down priorities (it could be right now!). What were the symptoms that life wasn't (or isn't) working?

GET THINKING

Watch the video for session five. Use the outline provided to note any thoughts or concepts that stand out to you.

NOTES

At the end of the 2003 season, the Raiders were 4 – 12 and tied for the worst record in the NFL. When the next year's training camp began, Tim found out his sixteen years with the Raiders were coming to an end.

After relocating once, and then a year later being offered a job that would involve moving again, Tim chose to put his family first and end his football career.

"If you continually ask yourself what is important now, you won't waste time on the trivial."

Lou Holtz

The Bible makes it clear that our top priority needs to be the kingdom of God. We must love God with all our heart, soul, strength, and mind.

Jesus' friends Mary and Martha are a good illustration of the need to choose the right priorities. We must never get so busy "doing" — like Martha — that we don't spend time with Christ and listen to His words — like Mary.

As Gale Sayers used to say, "I am third": the Lord first, family and friends second, and ourselves third.

Spending time with his family after retirement gave Tim a chance to be different than his dad and really build into his kids.

The premature birth of Tim's first daughter, Timon, and his wife passing out from dehydration confronted Tim with the possibility of losing someone he loved. It reestablished his priorities quickly. Tough moments force us to see what truly matters.

WORTH REPEATING

"God wants to be at the forefront of our lives. He won't accept second place or half-hearted devotion to Him."

"To be successful in life, a man has to have his priorities in order."

"The influence I have on my kids is powerful. For better and worse, it may extend for generations."

"Maybe that's one reason why God allows us to go through so many tough moments. It forces us to see what truly matters."

GET TALKING

For most of us men, the enemy of the good is not the bad; our downfall is the good getting in the way of the *best*. It's not bad to lead full, productive lives with busy schedules; it's just that too often we mess up our priorities. We spend huge amounts of time at work, or pursue enjoyable but consuming hobbies, or even get immersed in worthy causes — all at the cost of our families and our relationship with God. Living at such a hectic pace keeps us from caring for our souls. Our connectedness with God suffers if we do not surrender to God's priorities.

> "Living in the light of eternity changes your priorities."
>
> Rick Warren

1. On your own, take no more than three or four minutes to shade in the following pie chart to roughly estimate a typical week — 168 hours — of your life (each segment = 8 hours). Label each area, using the categories provided, or add others that apply. (For example: The average person sleeps 8 hours per night, or 56 hours per week, so label 7 of the segments "rest/sleep.")

Categories of Ways I Use My Time

- Rest/sleep
- Job
- Family obligations
- Church
- Education/classes

- Personal spiritual development
- Time with friends
- Hobbies
- TV/Internet
- Other

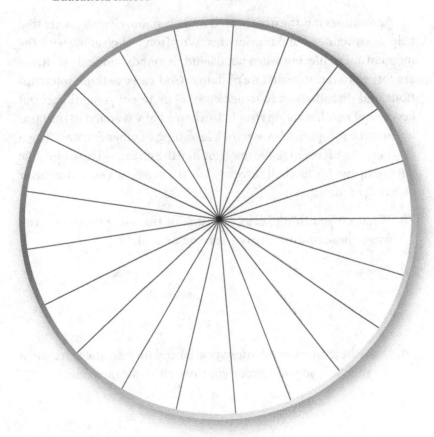

What is your reaction when you see the ways in which you use your time? Is there an area in which you would like to make a change?

2. Do you think it's possible to live a "balanced" life? Why or why not?

Sometimes it is the unexpected and even unwelcome events that help us straighten out our priorities. We often just go along with the momentum of life, but when needs and demands suddenly shift, we are forced to rethink what we're doing. God can use those interruptions and disturbances to either compel us to cut some things out because of new limitations (such as when a baby is added to the family) or open up options because of a lessening of other demands (such as when a layoff occurs). We may not like the chaos — Tim didn't like having to end his football career — but the crisis can lead to a better ordering of priorities.

3. What do you think keeps us stuck in the same routines, even when those routines are not serving us well?

4. Describe a time when an unexpected and unwelcomed change in your life helped you reorder your priorities for the better.

"It is not enough to be busy; so are the ants.
The question is, 'What are we busy about?'"
Henry David Thoreau

How has that change continued to affect you to this day? In what ways have you returned to some of your old priorities?

GET INSIGHT

5. The Bible contains many teachings about the brevity yet sacredness of life and the need to use our lives wisely and well. **Read** Psalm 90:10 – 12. Why do you think reflecting on the length of our lives will help us have hearts that are wise?

6. What will keep us from slipping into a gloomy outlook when we have such thoughts? (Verse 14 hints at one possibility, but you can probably think of others.)

7. Read Mark 8:34 – 37. How would you put into your own words Jesus' paradoxical statement that if we try to save our lives we will lose them?

What part of gaining the whole world is a temptation for you?

8. In what ways do you feel like you're losing the health of your soul even now because of how you're living? What do you think would help you regain that part of your soul?

"What counts can't always be counted;
what can be counted doesn't always count."
William Bruce Cameron

GET GOING

Pair up with another man in your group. You will each take turns doing this exercise. Begin by agreeing that each of you are willing to speak some hard truths and hear hard truths for the purpose of "gaining your soul" back in the way Jesus intends. Make sure you both are willing to do this, and then decide who will go first.

Start by asking the other person to summarize what he has heard from you during this meeting — or based on anything else he knows about you — that would describe how well you seem to know and live your priorities. You are not to respond in any way other than to ask a clarifying question or say, "Thank you, is there anything else?" The man who is sharing his opinions about you is not to give advice or say what you should do — he is simply diagnosing and giving his observations. Do not defend or explain; just receive this man's assessment of you as his point of view, even if you think he doesn't have all the facts.

Next, mirror back what you heard the other person say. Make sure that when you summarize his assessment of you, he believes you have heard him correctly. If he thinks you've missed a point or added in something he didn't say, have him restate his point of view and then mirror it back again until he knows you have heard him correctly.

When you are finished, complete this sentence: "What I think God is telling me to do as a result of all this is _____ _____." Do not go into a lot of storytelling, try to justify yourself, or make aspirations. Simply state concisely a measurable action step that you want to take for yourself.

Now switch roles. Have the other person be the one to receive feedback from you, and conclude with his resolution. When both of you have shared, end in prayer for each other to take action on what you've committed to do.

Between-Sessions Personal Study

Complete the following personal study on your own sometime between now and your next group meeting. It's best to not try to finish it all at once but do it over a few sittings to give yourself time to mull over what you're studying.

READ AND REFLECT

Read chapter 17, "A Man Knows His Priorities," and chapter 18, "A Father Leads His Children," in *The Making of a Man* book. Use the space below to write any key points or questions you want to bring to the next group meeting.

REVIEW AND STUDY

1. Look over the video outline and your notes from the group study. What is the "big idea" you want to take away? It may be a quote, a new way of looking at an issue, a reminder of a forgotten lesson, or something you sense God wants you to do. Note that here:

2. One way to organize your activities so they align with the right priorities is to think of your whole life as a mission. What big and audacious goal have you set for yourself? It isn't that you are going to reach it perfectly, because by definition a mission needs to be bigger than what you can accomplish, but it will give you direction and allow you to move toward worthy objectives. It will also help you eliminate good but less important activities if they don't line up with your mission.

3. Read Luke 4:16–21. How would you summarize Jesus' mission statement based on this passage?

Next, **read** Luke 19:10 and Mark 10:45. In these two passages, Jesus puts His mission statement even more succinctly. Combine these two texts into one mission statement.

4. Now think about your own mission. Jot down some phrases below that capture what you want your life to be about. Make sure that at least some of the things you write are so big you couldn't possibly finish them in your lifetime.

Look over the following list of action words. Circle 7 – 10 that fit you well.

accomplish	confirm	enlist	integrate	prepare	sell
acquire	connect	enliven	involve	present	serve
administer	consider	entertain	keep	produce	share
adopt	construct	enthuse	know	progress	speak
advance	contact	envision	labor	promise	stand
affect	continue	evaluate	launch	promote	summon
affirm	counsel	excite	lead	provide	support
alleviate	create	explore	live	realize	surrender
amplify	decide	express	make	receive	sustain
appreciate	defend	extend	manifest	reclaim	take
ascend	delight	facilitate	master	reduce	tap
associate	deliver	finance	mature	refine	team
believe	demonstrate	forgive	measure	reflect	touch
bestow	devise	foster	mediate	reform	trade
brighten	direct	franchise	model	regard	translate
build	discover	further	mold	relate	travel
call	discuss	gather	motivate	relax	understand
cause	distribute	generate	move	release	uphold
choose	draft	give	negotiate	rely	use
claim	dream	grant	nurture	remember	utilize
collect	drive	heal	open	renew	validate
combine	educate	hold	organize	resonate	value
command	elect	host	participate	respect	venture
communicate	embrace	identify	pass	restore	verbalize
compel	encourage	ignite	perform	return	volunteer
compete	endow	illuminate	persuade	revise	work
complete	engage	implement	play	sacrifice	worship
compliment	engineer	improve	possess	safeguard	write
compose	enhance	improvise	practice	satisfy	yield
conceive	enlighten	inspire	praise	save	

We'll push "pause" for now and come back to develop your mission statement a bit later in the study.

5. Some people imagine that a mission of which God approves would be exhausting, painful, and/or tedious. As you look up each of the following verses, comment on how they speak to what kind of mission God most likely has for you:

• Matthew 6:25 – 33

• Matthew 11:28 – 30

• John 10:10

• Romans 12:2

• Ephesians 2:10

• Philippians 2:13

6. List below some of the activities you do that renew, refresh, and build you up spiritually. Are there any that you would like to do more of in the short term?

"Whenever I feel like I'm getting too far away from where I need to be, I think about my sons and the legacy I have to leave for them — and it always brings me back to reality."

Dwayne Wade

---

7. From the passages below, what are some core spiritual practices that Jesus models and the Bible advises us to engage in?

• Acts 2:42

• Matthew 4:4

• 1 Peter 2:2

• Acts 17:11

- 1 Timothy 2:1 – 3, 8

• Philippians 4:6 – 7

• Luke 5:16

• Mark 6:31

Why do you think these activities are so important to our spiritual life?

8. In Matthew 6:33, Jesus is clear about what is to be the top priority in our lives. What do you think this means, practically speaking, in your life; in other words, what does a day look like when you put God's kingdom before all other activities?

9. God gives all of us talents and abilities that we are to use in His service. We are not all the same, and it is good that our differences exist! What insight does Paul give in 1 Corinthians 12:12 – 27 about God's plan in this regard?

What core talents and abilities has God given *you*? (Note: Do not compare your value to any other person — just acknowledge who and what you are as gifts from God.)

"The chief cause of failure and unhappiness is trading what you want most for what you want now."

Zig Ziglar

---

10. What do you hope those who love you most and know you best will say about you at your funeral? What legacy do you want to leave?

11. Now let's bring your mission back into focus. Using all that you have learned during the group time as well as your own individual study time, complete the following phrase starters:

I want my life to be about… (summarize your phrases from question 4)

Utilizing these strengths… (use your top two or three key action words, also from question 4)

Using my God-given abilities to … (summarize the second part of your answer to question 9)

So that… (list the aspects of God's kingdom that your efforts will help build)

12. Now put everything together using what you have written down and create a concise mission statement for your life.

A Man Builds a Godly Legacy

GET TOGETHER

Begin your time together by having each group member complete the following icebreaker sentence:

An interesting thing I've been told about my relatives a few generations back is _____

_____.

GET THINKING

Watch the video for session six. Use the outline provided to note any thoughts or concepts that stand out to you.

NOTES

The first place a boy looks to figure out what it means to be a man is his dad. Tim reminds his son that he is the man of the house in his father's absence, and even though he's only a boy, he takes that role seriously.

Tim's dad, who never missed work, had a huge influence on Tim's life. He died at seventy-five and had a well-attended funeral fit for a head of state because of all the people on which he had an impact.

"We stand our best chance of leaving a legacy to those who want to learn—our children—by standing firm. In matters of style, swim with the stream; in matters of principle, stand like a rock."
Author unknown

Although Tim misses his dad, he is grateful that "Mother Page," a woman from his church, heard a word from God to call his dad and pray with him over the phone. The night before he died, Tim's dad told Tim's mom that he was "all right with God."

Six months after the death of Tim's father, his buddy Chester, who was only forty-two years old, had a massive heart attack and also died. Tim became acutely aware that no one knows how long we have on earth, and nothing truly lasts.

The purpose of life isn't our achievements; we're called to serve God. That's what lasts.

In the Bible, Moses understood the importance of leaving a legacy, and he trained young Joshua to be a leader. It takes deliberate effort to pass along values to the next generation.

As fathers, we should not try to be "buddies" with our kids. They need clear guidance, and we need to be leaders who may have to tell them things they don't like. Sometimes, we have to be the no-fun parent.

Our sons are always watching us. Though we are their heroes, they also learn about our not-so-good qualities.

When we reach the end of our lives, we will be remembered for the good we did, the love we gave our families, and for how we honored God and did His will.

Like Paul wrote to Timothy, we should hope to be able to say, "I have fought the good fight, I have finished the race, I have kept the faith. Now there is in store for me the crown of righteousness" (2 Timothy 4:7 – 8).

WORTH REPEATING

"Every boy dreams of growing up to be a man ... The first place he's going to look is his dad."

"The reason I'm on this earth is to serve God; to be the best husband, father, son, brother, and friend I can be; and to lead people to Christ. These are the things that matter. These are the things that truly last."

"I want to be remembered as a guy who was faithful to God and was consistent in the way he lived and served others. If at the end of my days I see each member of my family honoring God and doing His will, I will know that I have created a legacy of which I can be proud."

GET TALKING

1. What do you think about when you hear the phrase "Be a man"? Some aspects of manhood we all likely think are the same; other aspects we may view differently. Take a few minutes to fill in the following chart with a few key words or short phrases, and then compare your answers with everyone in the group.

Being a man means ...
Most men will say ...
More men *should* say ...
Jesus would say ...

My dad taught me that a man is ...
The good things he modeled ...
What he was missing ...
Wounds from him I still carry ...

(cont.)

How I measure up as a man ...

What I'm getting right ...

What I need to do better ...

What I'm confused about ...

The question of whether or not you will leave a legacy has already been answered: for better or for worse, you will permanently affect those closest to you through what you do or don't do. The question is *what kind* of legacy you are leaving. Is it a godly legacy — the kind you *want* to leave? Will your kids look back on your life and see you as a role model and an example to live by? Or will they end up in a counselor's office for months — maybe years — trying to work through the hurt they feel you did to them, either through your presence or your neglect? What will your wife remember most about you when you are gone? Will your friends jaw about all the good times you had — yet be no better off as men, husbands, or fathers because you made no impact whatsoever on their character?

"We knew once the Creation was broken, true fathering would be much more lacking than mothering. Don't misunderstand me, both are needed — but an emphasis on fathering is necessary because of the enormity of its absence."
William Paul Young, *The Shack*

2. Tim Brown said the plaque his family put on his dad's casket simply read, "Patriarch." It summed up what he meant to them. Someday, you will lie in a casket, and your family may choose a plaque for you. What will it say? What one word or phrase will sum up what you meant to them?

3. What are a few words or phrases that represent the legacy you want to leave for your family?

What are some of the ways you have built that legacy? What else would you like to do to make it even better?

GET INSIGHT

As Tim mentioned, our children are watching us all the time. They are picking up who we are — not when we're trying to be good, but when we're going about daily life. They see what we're like and what's important to us through the actions we take when we think no one is looking. As Blaise Pascal wrote, "The strength of a man's virtue should not be measured by his special exertions but by his habitual acts." Our children watch our routines, not our exceptional acts. That's how they judge the kind of dad they have.

4. **Read** Deuteronomy 6:5 – 9. Some dads think they should leave their children's spiritual instruction to the "experts" in a Christian school or church. Those individuals are certainly valuable, but according to this passage what is the primary conduit through which children are to learn God's commandments? And why do you think that is the most important place for kids to be taught?

5. Practically speaking, what do you think it means to put God's commands on your hands, foreheads, doorposts, and gates?

In what ways do you do that? In what ways would you like to do more of that?

6. While many passages in the New Testament teach us about being a good person, only a few are aimed at being a good dad. One key passage is Ephesians 6:4, in which Paul says, "Fathers, do not exasperate your children; instead, bring them up in the training and instruction of the Lord." This text has two parts: (1) a prohibition, or what we are *not* to do, and (2) an exhortation, or what we should *actively* do. How would you summarize those two commands in your own words?

Of all the actions or behaviors on which fathers might focus, why do you think the apostle Paul stresses these two?

How do you need help with the first part of the command? How do you need help accomplishing the latter?

"In the end, it doesn't matter how well we have performed or what we have accomplished—a life without heart is not worth living."

John Eldredge

GET GOING

Answer the following reflection questions on your own. If you are not a father, use another relationship as the focus.

My biggest parenting failure is ...

What I need to do to make amends concerning that is ...

What I do that angers my children (in an unhealthy way) is ...

I could encourage my children more by ...

I would like to appreciate my wife for ...

I want to be a better influence on the men in my life by ...

Pair up with another man. Share your answers, and pray for each other that you can leave a better legacy through these initiatives. Then, as time permits, gather again as a large group to close *The Making of a Man* study in prayer.

Final Personal Study

Complete the following personal study on your own sometime in the coming days. It's best to not try to finish it all at once but do it over a few sittings to give yourself time to mull over what you're studying.

READ AND REFLECT

Read chapter 16, "Little Things Lead to Big Results," and chapter 20, "Your Legacy Matters," in *The Making of a Man* book. Use the space below to write any key points or questions you want to discuss with a friend or fellow group member in the near future.

1. Look over the video outline and your notes from the group study. What is the "big idea" you want to take away? It may be a quote, a new way of looking at an issue, a reminder of a forgotten lesson, or something you sense God wants you to do. Note that here:

2. What are some of the best qualities your father had that you also see in your life?

3. For what would he be most proud of you?

4. How would you like to go beyond your father's legacy and be an even better man?

5. Read Exodus 20:12 and Matthew 19:19. God tells us that we are to honor our fathers, yet our dads are imperfect people and some of them may have wounded us deeply. Many men do not even know their fathers. How do you think it is possible for a man to be honest about the pain his father's sin caused and yet at the same time still honor him?

"Be more concerned with your character than your reputation, because your character is what you really are, while your reputation is merely what others think you are."
John Wooden

How would you want your children to deal with the wrong that you did to them? What insight does that give you on how to honor parents while at the same time dealing honestly with their failures?

6. A legacy is not just a matter of doing right by way of our children. We also leave a legacy in how we do our jobs, influence our friends' lives, impact the next generation of young leaders, and make the world a better place. **Read** the following verses and comment on how they apply to your own legacy-making.

• Psalm 127:1 – 2

• Matthew 5:14 – 16

• Matthew 6:19 – 21

• Luke 9:23 – 25

(cont.)

• Colossians 3:17

• Colossians 3:23 – 24

• Colossians 4:5 – 6

7. When Paul was placed in prison in Rome, he had a sense that he soon would be martyred. As he reflected back on his life, he wrote a letter to Timothy, his young protégé. Among his "last words," so to speak, were these: "I have fought the good fight, I have finished the race, I have kept the faith" (2 Timothy 4:7). Like Paul, what is "the good fight" you need to fight with your life? What do you think will happen if you don't win that fight?

What "race" have you started that you need to finish? What do you think will be your reward for finishing it well?

What threats or doubts might prevent you from "keeping the faith"? How can you strengthen your faith so that doesn't happen?

8. Just before Jesus died, he declared, "It is finished" (John 19:30). The work His Father gave Him to do—everything leading up to the cross, and the cross itself—had been completed. In a world of need, there was always more He *could* have done. After all, there were still sick people to heal, lost people to save, and villages He hadn't visited. But somehow, Jesus knew the essential work of *His* life was done. Others would have to take up the baton to bring the kingdom of God to the ends of the earth.

What about you? As a result of what you've been learning through this study, what would you like to do in the coming weeks so that you can move toward being able to say, "It is finished," when you die?

> "Each day of our lives we make deposits in the memory banks of our children."
>
> **Charles Swindoll**